Emergency Request Justification
Department of State, Foreign Operations, and Related Programs

Contents

Overview

Since the first cases of Ebola Virus Disease (Ebola) were reported in West Africa in March 2014, the United States has mounted a whole-of-government response to contain and stop the spread of the virus, while also taking prudent measures at home. There are currently more than 1,350 U.S. government personnel on the ground in West Africa, making this the largest-ever U.S. response to a global health crisis. The World Health Organization (WHO) projects that it will take at least six months to bring the outbreak under control. The goal of the United States in West Africa is to stop the epidemic at its source through mobilizing our government-wide capabilities to fight the epidemic on a regional basis. The Ebola crisis is derailing not only lives, but livelihoods, in some of the most vulnerable communities in the world. Fears of infection have disrupted normal economic activity in West Africa. If the epidemic is not contained during 2015, this cost will multiply nearly ten-fold.

The requested funding will enhance the Administration's current whole-of-government response to help end the Ebola outbreak in West Africa and support increased domestic preparedness. The U.S. Agency for International Development (USAID) and the Centers for Disease Control and Prevention (CDC) and are partnering to lead U.S. government efforts to address the Ebola outbreak in West Africa. These agencies have a history of working together, including for the past 10 years in Africa. Building on this foundation, USAID and CDC will lead a coordinated effort against Ebola based on each agency's unique technical capabilities and comparative advantage. CDC is the Nation's public health agency and possesses the technical skills and capacity needed to respond effectively to epidemic threats and large-scale public health emergencies. CDC understands this crisis will require the resources and ingenuity that many Departments and Agencies, as well as NGOs, ministries of health and multilateral organizations offer. USAID is the lead federal agency for overseas disaster response and is mandated through the Foreign Assistance Act to provide development assistance and disaster response. USAID has a long history of rapid deployment and scaling up of assistance in crisis environments and expertise in supporting the efforts of the U.S. government through a variety of partners. USAID and CDC are working together through the Disaster Assistance Response Team (DART) structure to ensure coordination and collaboration on technical and operational matters.

USAID and the Department of State are mobilizing more than $200 million as part of an initial response, but additional resources, including the potential replenishment of funds already used, are required through September 2015 to control the outbreak, mitigate second order impacts, build coherent leadership and operations, strengthen the global health security response, and advance the Global Health Security Agenda (GHSA).

The request allows funds appropriated to be transferred across accounts within the Department of State and USAID as necessary to provide the most appropriate responses to the Ebola epidemic. The request also allows accounts to be reimbursed for funding that was expended to help stem the Ebola epidemic and prevent an even more rapid spread of the disease prior to the enactment of the emergency appropriation.

Ebola Base

The request includes $2.1 billion for USAID and State to respond to the Ebola crisis in West Africa ($1.8 billion) and advance the GHSA ($278 million).

$1.8 billion specifically for Ebola response is focused on controlling the outbreak, addressing urgent humanitarian needs, mitigating second order impacts, and supporting operations requirements. Funding will support medical and non-medical management of Ebola treatment units (ETU) and community care centers (CCC), which are specially designed medical facilities to care for patients suffering from Ebola and complement the ETUs; provide ETU and CCC facilities with personal protective equipment (PPE) and supplies; expand the number of safe burial teams; support the recruitment and sustainment of international healthcare workers; fund a regional logistics network to support the international response; expand the reach of contact tracing and infection control systems and protocols into rural areas and through expanded training platforms for healthcare professionals; scale up social mobilization and community education efforts critical to preventing the spread of the disease; fund emergency health services, health systems recovery, and address other second-order impacts on health systems, such as adverse effects on maternal and child health; and address food insecurity and other second-order impacts in governance, economic activity, and information and communication technology.

In addition, the request supports the use of traditional and non-traditional media sources such as radio and television, as well as messaging in local languages, for public outreach and delivery of educational information, in order to message best practices on the prevention and treatment of Ebola. The request also ensures the health and safety of both existing U.S. government personnel and emergency response personnel.

$278 million for global health security activities will prevent emerging diseases from spreading, report threats in real-time, and establish needed capability for expert personnel and equipment to stop health emergencies before they become epidemics. This will help limit the spread of Ebola and other dangerous pathogens beyond Liberia, Sierra Leone, and Guinea to other vulnerable nations and will increase preparedness and response capacity for future outbreaks.

Contingency Fund

$792 million for the Contingency Fund will ensure that resources are available to respond to the evolving Ebola outbreak. Activities may include a larger scale Ebola response in Liberia, Guinea, Sierra Leone, and other affected countries, if necessary, based on the trajectory of the epidemic. Funds could also support the recovery of health systems and economies from the outbreak, including by enhancing the capacity of the governments and security institutions to manage the impact of the crisis. If necessary, the Contingency Fund could also support increased domestic efforts here in the United States.

Summary Tables

Accounts ($ in thousands)	FY 2013 Actual	FY 2014 Estimate	FY 2015 Request (As Amended as of 11/5/2014)	FY 2015 Emergency Request	FY 2015 Revised Request
Total	**12,373,112**	**11,398,919**	**19,705,193**	**2,896,381**	**22,601,574**
International Disaster Assistance (IDA)	1,550,395	1,801,000	1,300,000	1,400,973	2,700,973
Global Health Programs – USAID (GHP-USAID)	2,626,059	2,769,450	2,680,000	340,000	3,020,000
Economic Support Funds (ESF)	5,867,473	4,589,182	5,077,094	211,725	5,288,819
International Organizations and Programs (IO&P)	326,651	344,020	303,439	50,300	353,739
Nonproliferation, Antiterrorism, Demining and Related Programs (NADR)	674,862	700,000	605,400	5,300	610,700
USAID Operating Expenses (OE)	1,279,251	1,140,229	1,383,816	19,037	1,402,853
USAID Office of Inspector General (IG)	48,421	55,038	54,285	5,626	59,911
Diplomatic & Consular Programs (D&CP)	6,467,426	6,617,625	6,782,510	35,420	6,817,930
Contributions to International Organizations (CIO)	1,376,338	1,265,762	1,517,349	35,000	1,552,349
Repatriation Loans Program	1,651	1,537	1,300	1,000	2,300
Ebola Contingency - Economic Support Funds (ESF)	-	-	-	792,000	792,000

Note: Of the $2.9 billion emergency request, $2.1 billion is for immediate response and $792 million is for the Contingency Fund.

Foreign Assistance by Account and Pillar

Pillars ($ in thousands)	Total	IDA	ESF	NADR	IO&P	USAID OE	USAID IG	GHP-USAID
Foreign Assistance Ebola Base	**2,032,961**	**1,400,973**	**211,725**	**5,300**	**50,300**	**19,037**	**5,626**	**340,000**
Pillar I - Control the Outbreak	1,264,448	1,194,848	14,000	5,300	50,300	-	-	-
Pillar II - Mitigate Second Order Impacts	387,725	190,000	197,725	-	-	-	-	-
Pillar III - Coherent Leadership and Operations	40,788	16,125	-	-	-	19,037	5,626	-
Pillar IV - Global Health Security Response	62,000	-	-	-	-	-	-	62,000
Global Health Security Agenda	278,000	-	-	-	-	-	-	278,000

Diplomatic Engagement by Account and Pillar

Pillars ($ in thousands)	Total	D&CP	CIO	Repatriation Loans Program
Diplomatic Engagement	**71,420**	**35,420**	**35,000**	**1,000**
Supports Pillar I - Control the Outbreak	35,000	-	35,000	-
Supports Pillar III - Coherent Leadership and Operations	36,420	35,420	-	1,000

Foreign Assistance

Pillar I, Control the Outbreak ($1.3 billion):

Contact Tracing: ($25 million IDA)
Contact tracing is the process of identifying the relevant contacts of a person with an infectious disease and ensuring that the contacts are aware that they have been exposed. The U.S. government plans to support community health workers and volunteers to actively trace and follow up on non-symptomatic contacts, seek out symptomatic cases, and encourage symptomatic cases to seek immediate care. USAID partners work within countries' Ministries of Health (MoH) tracing structures to expand the scale and geographic reach of county-level health officials and community health workers. USAID – as needed and in close technical coordination with the CDC – will fund contact tracing activities through partners to ensure country-wide capacity. USAID will support CDC to provide complementary contact tracing activities through NGO partners. Both agencies work under a single national Incident Manager and perform contact tracing duties consistent with CDC and MoH technical guidance to ensure proper procedures for contact tracing are maintained. All partners (U.S. government, contractors, grantees, etc.) will coordinate their work with CDC. USAID expects to have at least 15 case investigation teams and nearly 1,600 contract tracers operational by the end of January.

Healthcare Workers ($27 million IDA; $5 million ESF)
The severe shortage of health staff trained in Ebola response techniques in affected countries has resulted in Ebola infections among health workers and patients unable to receive care. The U.S. government plans to support a range of efforts to address infections among healthcare workers and ensure a sufficient number of trained healthcare workers to staff ETUs and CCCs. This request will support the deployment of Commissioned Corps Officers from the U.S. Public Health Service, who will staff a specialized treatment center for healthcare workers who contract Ebola. Assistance will also support healthcare worker training in Liberia and Guinea to train all ETU and CCC staff beyond those trained by the Department of Defense (DoD). USAID expects to have 2,510 health care workers in Liberia trained and ready to staff ETUs by the end of January.

These funds will also add to continued U.S. government assistance to the African Union's (AU) African Union Support to Ebola Outbreak in West Africa (ASEOWA) program, by which the AU is deploying health care personnel to Ebola-stricken areas. These funds will be used for equipment, supplies, personnel, and transportation needs for ASEOWA.

Ebola Treatment Units ($539.2 million IDA; $4.5 million ESF)
ETUs are specially designed medical facilities to care for patients suffering from the Ebola Virus Disease (EVD). ETUs are essential to help break the chain of transmission of EVD – patients are treated outside of their communities in an isolated facility to prevent further infection of community and family members. Management of ETUs is divided into two categories: clinical support, which is the medical care for the patients; and non-medical management support, which covers the functions essential to the running of a facility such as an ETU. More than 25 ETUs are planned for Liberia. The United States plans to fund clinical and non-medical management at 19 ETUs. All U.S.-funded ETUs are targeted to be fully operational by the end of January.

Resources in this request will allow for the phased scaling of all ETUs operated by the U.S. government.

The operating costs of ETUs are extremely high due to costs of supplies, staffing support needs, and other factors. Working in coordination with CDC, a laboratory support network will organize and staff the safe transport of specimens for testing for EVD and communication of lab results. The more ETUs that are operational, the more patients with EVD that can be removed from their communities to receive treatment for the disease and help stop the further spread of EVD.

Community Care Centers ($208.2 million IDA; $4.5 million ESF)
The limited number of ETU beds has resulted in suspected EVD patients being treated at home. As partners continue to scale up ETUs, interim and complementary strategies are needed, such as CCCs. CCCs are intended to be basic, community-based structures where symptomatic individuals can be moved out of their homes to reduce household transmission while receiving safe, basic care from a household attendant under the direction of a trained health worker from a nearby health facility. The U.S. government plans to support up to 150 CCCs in Liberia as needed. By the end of January, at least 40 CCCs with nearly 1,000 beds will be completed.

Burial Teams ($36.8 million IDA)
The safe management of bodies infected with EVD is an essential component of stopping the spread of the disease, as infected bodies pose significant transmission risk. In order to assist with safe burials, the U.S. government will support a countrywide network of 65 safe burial teams in Liberia. In most counties of the country, burial teams and disinfection teams are active and in place. However, nearly all of these teams lack sufficient critical supplies such as personal protective equipment (PPEs), body bags, and chlorine for disinfection. They also lack the necessary resources to pay salaries and rent vehicles to reach remote areas to collect and bury Ebola victims. Without these resources and staff, bodies are left in homes and on streets, leading to the further risk of infection and transmission of the deadly virus. USAID will support burial teams to continue their efforts to combat the spread of Ebola and increase their capacity to respond and manage caseloads as a means of reducing threats to the surrounding community. Working with partners, the U.S. government-supported countrywide system will maintain a call center and aim to ensure that all calls for the safe burial of EVD victims are met within 24 hours in all 15 of Liberia's counties. Assistance also supports burial teams in Guinea and Sierra Leone. By the end of January, USAID expects to have 56 burial teams in place.

Health Services and Infection Control ($22.8 million IDA; $5.3 million NADR)
Health services funding will support the uninterrupted flow of PPEs to all non-Ebola healthcare facilities in-country; train health staff in non-Ebola health facilities on the triage/referral of Ebola patients to more appropriate facilities; and train government authorities, especially law enforcement, to mitigate disease risks caused by dangerous pathogens such as Ebola.

Activities will focus on infection control protocol training and commodity support to non-Ebola health facilities. Health staff will be specifically trained in how to manage interactions with suspected Ebola cases, minimize the risk of exposure to health workers, and protect patients from unintended exposure and possible infection. By the end of January all non-Ebola health facilities in the five most affected counties in Liberia would be trained in infection control protocols and have adequate supplies of PPEs.

The Department of State is currently working in West Africa to mitigate the crisis by providing support to local law enforcement, security services, and laboratory personnel to foster secure, safe, and effective outbreak management.

USAID funding for infection control will strengthen health systems by implementing a rapid scale up of infection control support to non-Ebola specific health facilities country-wide in Liberia. Using internationally approved protocols and policies, funding will support the training and provision of supplies to every non-Ebola health facility in Liberia, as well as provide quality assurance backstopping. This approach will enable an efficient and effective scaling up of infection control measures.

The following activities would be funded through allocations from the Nonproliferation, Antiterrorism, Demining, and Related Programs-Global Threat Reduction Program (NADR-GTR), which has unique expertise to secure dangerous pathogens such as Ebola and to train governmental authorities, especially law enforcement, to mitigate disease risks caused by the most dangerous pathogens:

Training of Law Enforcement and Security Forces to Guard Facilities that Store Ebola ($1.2 million NADR)
Funds will support a series of trainings for West African law enforcement officials to enhance their ability to impose quarantines and guard potentially hazardous facilities. The program will provide subject matter expertise, course materials, logistical support, and equipment/supply training resources, such as PPEs and related instruction. Trainings will bolster the capacity of local police forces to adequately contain the Ebola outbreak and provide regional stability in a crisis environment.

Training for Disposal of Hazardous Materials ($830,000 NADR)
These programs will train healthcare and laboratory workers on proper techniques for burying or otherwise destroying materials contaminated with the Ebola virus, thereby minimizing the possibility that Ebola will be illicitly obtained. These funds will support the deployment of infectious disease and biosecurity teams to facilitate the destruction and disinfection of contaminated materials that may otherwise be ignored during a chaotic pandemic scenario. Front-line staff will be trained and equipped to work securely in high containment settings to prevent the further spread of Ebola, to reduce the threat to regional security and stability, and to prevent access to especially dangerous pathogens.

Strengthening Emergency Preparedness Systems in At-Risk Countries ($1.7 million NADR)
Programs will strengthen laboratory capacity, biosecurity, and biosafety practices at priority facilities in West Africa to ensure response efforts are in place in at-risk countries. Côte d'Ivoire, Mali, and Senegal have been identified as priority countries for engagement given their proximity to Ebola hot zones. This funding would support risk assessments and diagnostic upgrades at laboratories to ensure West African regional

countries have the capability to rapidly detect, respond, and contain an outbreak in the event of the continued spread of this virus. This is especially relevant with the recent announcement of the first confirmed case of Ebola in Mali.

Promoting Biosecurity and Biosafety Practices in Hospital and Laboratory Environments ($1.6 million NADR)
Ensuring that front-line healthcare workers are fully prepared, equipped, and trained to securely and safely work in an isolation setting is crucial to preventing secondary infections in an outbreak scenario. Funds will leverage non-governmental biorisk management experts to train healthcare providers and other frontline responders in West Africa on how to securely and safely operate in contaminated environments. Providing this training will assist in controlling the spread of this outbreak to healthcare workers operating in this crisis environment.

Social Mobilization and Community Outreach ($66.9 million IDA)
The spread of Ebola within families and among community members is largely a function of individual behaviors that under normal situations are non-threatening, but in the presence of the EVD are highly risky. Traditional care giving and burial practices are known to be major drivers of the spread of the virus. Social Mobilization and Community Outreach activities are designed to disrupt transmission of the virus through communication campaigns to inform people across Ebola stricken communities on the risks associated with certain behaviors and the simultaneous promotion of alternative safe behaviors. In addition, this area of work will support the provision of household protection kits to be used by caregivers as an interim measure when individuals suspected of having Ebola are not able to be admitted to either an ETU or CCC and need home care. Funds will also be used to provide messaging and training for caregivers on the appropriate use of the home kits. This home-based care option, while not as effective as either the ETU or CCC in protecting against transmission, can provide measurable protection for household members and can dramatically reduce the overall rate of transmission of Ebola in the community when combined with ETU and CCC coverage. Resources will support messaging through new and traditional media (television, radio, newspapers), which will be combined with community dialogue efforts through community and religious leaders to reach across populations. By the end of January, USAID anticipates that four million people will have knowledge of Ebola and the key protective measures and that all deaths in communities/households are referred to government burial teams. And, if people suspected of Ebola are turned away from ETUs or CCCs for lack of space all of those individuals will receive home protection kits and training in how to use them.

Logistics, Systems, and Supplies ($269.1 million IDA)
As part of the U.S. response, USAID will procure and transport supplies, such as plastic sheeting, sprayers, and other materials, for Ebola response efforts. Assuming that DoD's mission set remains within the parameters currently defined by Operation United Assistance, does not include direct patient care, and would only last for 180 days, USAID will be providing support for a PPE pipeline to ensure that ETUs supported by the United States have an adequate supply of PPE to cover their needs. Specifically, the pipeline includes the procurement, transport, and warehousing of PPEs in 17 ETUs not covered by DoD beyond 4 months. For the remaining three ETUs, the request provides 12 months of support. This funding will also support the

creation of logistics hubs in the region – enabling organizations to transport, warehouse, and ultimately distribute needed supplies into remote areas. The PPEs for non-Ebola healthcare facilities are covered in the *"Health Services and Infection Control"* section.

Voluntary International Organization Contributions ($50.3 million, IO&P)

World Health Organization (WHO) Ebola Response Roadmap ($50 million IO&P)
WHO is integral to the broad United Nations (UN) system response. A contribution of $50 million toward an overall request by the Organization of $260 million will assist the WHO in achieving full implementation of its Ebola Response Roadmap, furthering its primary objectives to achieve full geographic coverage in affected countries, ensuring comprehensive Ebola response interventions, and strengthening preparedness in neighboring countries. Funds will allow WHO to continue to provide essential technical support for the overall coordination, surveillance, and data collection in each affected country; help governments establish ETUs and CCCs; train hundreds of health workers; establish exit screening; and coordinate UN-wide medical evacuation services. Funds will support mission-critical public health actions to identify and trace people with Ebola and support safe and dignified burials, care for persons with Ebola and infection control, medical care of responders, and access to basic health services. WHO and partner organizations have agreed on core actions to support non-affected countries in strengthening their preparedness and are collaborating actively in non-affected countries on the implementation of increased public health measures.

The U.S. government's Ebola Response strategy was developed in conjunction with the WHO Ebola Roadmap, which was incorporated into the UN's collective Ebola appeal. Bilateral support for the Ebola response - such as activities undertaken by USAID and CDC - is provided in coordination with this broader UN framework. Activities on the ground are undertaken with a multi-partner approach and are closely coordinated along geographic and technical lines based on comparative advantage. This voluntary contribution from IO&P funds would provide a general contribution directed to the WHO's Ebola appeal. On the ground, as the crisis evolves, the U.S. government is continuously coordinating with the host country governments and the UN to ensure un-earmarked UN contributions are utilized to meet the most urgent unmet needs,

UNMEER is working to ensure a singular and coherent response in the three affected countries. UNMEER and the WHO responsibilities within the UNMEER operational framework are designed as a response that pulls in the international community as a whole to work together in a coordinated and coherent manner.

WHO will continue be a critical player in the preparedness, health interventions, data collection and analysis and reporting.

International Civil Aviation Organization (ICAO), Management of Public Health Events in Civil Aviation ($300,000 IO&P)
This program will support training in countries impacted by Ebola for civil aviation staff in international airports to implement sound screening procedures for the virus. ICAO works closely with CDC, WHO, and the impacted West African nations (all of which are ICAO members) to build capacity to respond to Ebola within the civil aviation community.

Note: Additional support for complementary Diplomatic Engagement programs in Pillar I is described separately in the Diplomatic Engagement section.

<u>Pillar II, Mitigate Second Order Impacts ($387.7 million)</u>:

<u>Food Security ($190 million IDA)</u>
USAID's Famine Early Warning Systems Network (FEWSNet) has flagged several major threats to food security resulting from Ebola over the coming months. These include a reduction in the current harvest and next season's planting due to quarantine rules and loss of productive labor; the loss of livelihoods due to the closure of businesses, schools, transportation services, etc.; and market disruptions and closures – resulting in rising food prices as well as increasingly constrained availability of and access to food and agricultural inputs. Driven by stressed and crisis stages in Ebola-affected communities, emergency levels of integrated food insecurity classification (IPC) Phase 4 are expected by March 2015. Based on this analysis and CDC projections, USAID's Office of Food for Peace (FFP) is mobilizing efforts to respond to the urgent food needs of 1.3 to 2 million people in Ebola-affected countries in FY 2015.

Working through the World Food Program and non-governmental partners, FFP will provide targeted, in-kind food rations to affected households and communities cut off from markets, as well as specialized food commodities to meet the expected need for supplementary feeding and institutional feeding required by Ebola treatment clinics, orphanages, and other specialized feeding programs.

<u>Regional Governance, Economic Crisis Mitigation, Information and Communication Technology, and Innovation ($71.7 million ESF)</u>
USAID programs in Liberia, Guinea, and the broader region will address the current and potential second-order impacts in Ebola-affected countries and critical innovations. The affected countries are absorbing a sharp reduction in the population's access to education and health services due to school closures and the collapse of staffing in non-Ebola health facilities. Unlike reduced investments in physical capital, the impacts of this interruption in human capital investment are not fully reversible.

USAID will support programs that address the potentially sharp increase in extreme poverty and food insecurity, including the welfare effects of the immediate loss of jobs and other income opportunities for vulnerable households. Funding will support critical power and transportation infrastructure investments that address key constraints in trade and access to basic services, including power and feeder road infrastructure investments. These infrastructure investments will support key investments that have languished as companies have re-located their expatriate staff and will support employment generation activities as the private investment and trade environment continues to deteriorate as a result of health risks. Investments in education programs will address the prolongation of severe human capacity gaps and weaknesses due to the indefinite closure of all educational institutions.

Of this amount, $10 million will support programs designed to make monthly cash transfers to the most vulnerable populations. Additional funding will support education programs targeted at re-opening schools and improving the conditions of these schools with hygiene and hand washing stations to assuage community concerns around contracting Ebola in large settings. While schools remain closed, USAID programming will support radio programs for primary and secondary school aged students while providing teacher training to address key gaps in pedagogy, literacy, and numeracy.

The request also includes an investment in the Information and Communications Technology (ICT) sector to fill critical emergency needs for communications as well as bolster infrastructure for a potential future crisis. Better communications through ICT investments will enable improved information flow to allow better decision making and resourcing to combat this emergency, as well as foster economic opportunity that comes from a robust information economy. Activities include funding technical advisors to identify barriers to maintaining telecommunications networks and infrastructure, software systems used for response, coordination and social mobilization, and digital payment infrastructure. Advisors will work with host country governments, and responders on the ground, to overcome barriers. As USAID addresses these issues, USAID will continue governance efforts that address the weak capacity of government institutions to address these shocks.

Bringing new ideas and technologies to increase the speed and efficiency of recovery is essential. Funding innovation in this context would enable rapid testing and data collection around new point-of-care solutions such as Personal Protective Equipment, Rapid Diagnostics and other technologies that aid in care and epidemiological study. Funding would also build out data capacity, including the collection of data in the region through novel means, the analysis and use of data for reporting and to inform action and the dissemination of data. Our focus would cover data that measures the impact of our aid in country, managerial data, such as inventory levels, workforce and others, research and scientific data for the impacted region, and the use of big data and analytics to understand more about the second-order impacts of our work. This funding request also includes a Grand Challenge to inspire quick and innovative improvements in PPE and Ebola control to improve the global response in the coming weeks and months.

Regional Emergency Non-Ebola Health Services ($60 million ESF)
Working closely with partner governments and other donors, USAID will ensure that basic health services are accessible to those most in need. Due to the devastating impact of Ebola on local health service delivery systems, Liberia, in particular, Sierra Leone, and Guinea will require external support to re-establish and sustain routine health services delivery. Activities will focus on restoring and strengthening service delivery and providing the technical assistance needed to rebuild sustainable capacity, including activities to address adverse effects on maternal and child health. By the end of January, USAID plans to have fully assessed service capacity and basic health services restoration plans in Liberia, Sierra Leone, and Guinea.

Regional Health Systems Recovery ($66 million ESF)
To address the longer-term recovery of health systems in Ebola-affected countries, USAID will make core investments in rebuilding the health workforce, strengthening core health systems functions, and ensuring that USAID Missions are staffed to manage programs geared to the restoration of health systems. To rebuild, expand, and improve the skill-base of health workers in these countries, USAID will join other partners to strengthen curriculum, teaching, and infrastructure at pre-service training institutions, and recruit and train faculty to develop a generation of new and better-trained clinicians and health managers. USAID will also address urgent priorities in the areas of health workforce systems, including hiring, compensation, and

motivation of staff. Other activities will include strengthening health sector governance, pharmaceutical management and commodity logistics, communications and routine information systems, quality improvement, laboratory systems, and health financing. By the end of January, a national health workforce development strategy will be drafted as well as the implementation of a national rapid assessment for core health systems functions.

Pillar III, Coherent Leadership and Operations ($40.8 million):

An effective U.S. government Ebola response requires coherent leadership and operations. In West Africa, U.S. government response efforts are coordinated through the USAID DART, which is supported from Washington by the Response Management Team (RMT). Given the unprecedented scale of the Ebola epidemic and U.S. government response, resources are needed to support the DART and RMT, as well as West Africa missions, the USAID Ebola Secretariat, and USAID bureaus.

Disaster Assistance Response Team and Response Management Team Operations ($16.1 million IDA)

The requested funding is required for program support and operational platforms, including the USAID DART and RMT. The DART and RMT coordinate with interagency partners in the field and Washington, other donors, governments of affected countries, and implementers. The DART has nearly doubled in size since the first deployment in September, requiring increased RMT staffing to provide support. This funding will enable continued scale-up in Guinea and facilitate scale-up in other countries as needed. In addition, the complexity and scale of the Ebola response has highlighted the need for additional direct hire staff; thus, the request includes funding for 20 additional OE-funded staff to ensure adequate readiness to support large-scale emergencies and manage contracts and grants. The request also includes funding to accommodate the increased demand on existing operational and program support mechanisms.

USAID Missions, Ebola Task Force, and Washington Support ($19.0 million OE)

To support the response to the Ebola crisis in Africa, USAID is requesting salaries, benefits, travel, and ancillary costs for temporary U.S. personnel, contractors, and additional travel, as well as for other costs for existing direct hire staff in both West Africa and the United States. USAID will primarily use the funds to support and hire USAID staff in Liberia, Guinea, Senegal, and the West Africa Regional program. In addition, funding will cover surge support and technical expertise in the United States. These U.S.-based staff will provide programmatic, technical, contracting, financial management, budget, and administrative support. The resources are required to support the significant increase in program management in both the field and Washington and provide the surge support needed to meet the new demands that the Ebola response creates.

USAID Office of Inspector General (OIG) ($5.6 million USAID OIG)

Utilizing current audit staff in Washington, Dakar, Senegal, as well as staff in other regions, and supplementing that staff with contracted-out audit firms and subject matter experts (in Health, Engineering, and Disaster Assistance), USAID's Office of Inspector General (OIG) will perform the following oversight in Guinea, Liberia, Sierra Leone, and any other locations where USAID manages or implements its Ebola programs:

Overseas Contingency Operations (OCO): If an OCO is formally declared, there is a high probability that the USAID OIG will be assigned the lead IG role. The lead IG role in an OCO will require staff for congressionally mandated planning, reporting and outreach related to the oversight activities of the OIGs for USAID and the Departments of Defense and State.

Fraud Awareness and Accountability Training and Assistance to Non-Federal Auditors: Assistance projects implemented in developing countries are at significant risk of fraud, waste, and abuse. To help address these risks, OIG staff will provide USAID officials, implementing partner staff, and local auditors with training and assistance (in regards to the audit firms) in identifying fraud, complying with the requirements of USAID contracts and agreements, and reporting potential violations to OIG.

Survey of USAID Ebola Assistance Activities: This survey will identify USAID's development activities in all affected countries and will assess the risks associated with those activities.

Audits of Selected USAID Ebola Activities: OIG will select USAID projects that are at high risk and will determine, through a series of audits, whether those activities are adequately progressing toward their objectives.

OIG's Office of Investigations anticipate that its staff will undertake a large-scale effort of outreach and education related to fraud and public corruption regarding this potentially pandemic healthcare issue. The outreach is necessary to develop sources of information and to maintain an understanding of the fraud risks in the operating environment. A successful education and outreach effort is likely to generate large volumes of healthcare/Ebola fraud allegations.

Note: Additional support for complementary Diplomatic Engagement programs in Pillar III is described separately in the Diplomatic Engagement section.

<u>Pillar IV, Global Health Security Response ($62.0 million GHP-USAID):</u>

<u>Preparedness activities in Ebola-affected countries of Liberia, Guinea, and Sierra Leone ($62 million GHP-USAID)</u>
These countries need to rapidly strengthen key aspects of preparedness (e.g. surveillance, laboratories, response, communications) to ensure rapid and effective action against emerging infectious diseases. USAID, in cooperation with WHO, CDC, and DoD, will assist these countries to not only prepare for Ebola, but also for outbreaks of diseases whose cause is not immediately known using a Public Health Emergency Framework previously developed by USAID, CDC, and WHO for countries in Central and East Africa. Using a "One Health" strategy, professionals from public health, medicine, veterinary medicine, and wildlife conservation will be engaged to strengthen their capacity to monitor and respond to animal viruses that may be public health threats.

The current Ebola epidemic vividly illustrates the perils of any country having weak disease prevention, detection, and response capacities, particularly in geographic areas where new public health threats are likely to emerge. USAID will provide support for disease surveillance, laboratories, rapid response teams, risk characterization, and risk-mitigation. As a part of the Ebola response, this funding will support immediate near-term activities to strengthen global health security preparedness. The Global Health Security Agenda will build upon this initial response and provide multi-year funding to strengthen capacity for preparedness, prevention, detection, and response in Africa, Asia, and the Americas.

<u>Global Health Security Agenda ($278 million GHP-USAID)</u>

<u>Preparing Unaffected Countries to Rapidly Detect and Control any Introduction of Ebola</u>:
The Ebola epidemic in West Africa has heightened awareness and concern about the preparedness systems necessary for managing the possible introduction of the Ebola virus into a previously unaffected country. Those countries within immediate proximity to Liberia, Sierra Leone, and Guinea are especially concerned about the virus crossing borders and further expanding and accelerating the spread. In our globalized world, however, no country is more than a flight away from a dangerous pathogen, as recently illustrated by the Ebola cases in Dallas and New York City.

Drawing on the lessons learned from ongoing efforts supported by USAID to assist countries in West Africa establish preparedness capabilities for the possible spread of the virus across their borders, this area of action will enable intensification of these efforts, as well as their expansion to include countries not immediately proximal to the ongoing Ebola epidemic. Central to this work is the development and testing of national Ebola Preparedness Plans. Using a combination of regional planning meetings, web-based training, and direct country level technical assistance countries will be able to develop and test national Ebola Preparedness and Response Plans.

<u>Preventing and Reducing the Threat of Future Outbreaks</u>:
The Ebola epidemic currently unfolding in West Africa is an unfortunate consequence of a region being ill-prepared to respond to a disease threat never previously detected in that part of Africa. Since it was first detected in 1977, the Ebola virus had previously been found only in Central and East Africa. Like other dangerous viral threats, the Ebola virus largely circulates in wild animal populations and on occasion "spills over" into humans taking a high toll in human life. These "spill over" events, however, are predictable and their impact need not be as dramatic as what we are witnessing in West Africa. What is required to limit the consequences of the "spill over" of Ebola and other highly dangerous pathogens, such as SARS, avian influenzas and the more recent Middle East Respiratory Syndrome (MERS) coronavirus, is to have in place a capacity to routinely monitor for the presence of these dangerous pathogens in animal populations and a linked system for early detection of their "spill over" into human populations and their rapid containment.

Since 2005, USAID has supported the routine monitoring of dangerous new animal pathogens and put in place capacities for their rapid detection and control. This work, which has proven highly effective in reducing the risk of the "spill over" and spread of new threats, has been targeted to a limited number of geographic "hot spots" in Central/East Africa and South East Asia. The resources requested in this line item will be used to build on this success and expand into other "hot spots" in West Africa, the Arabia Peninsula of the Middle East, and the Amazon region of South America, while intensifying efforts in Central/East Africa and South East Asia.

Diplomatic Engagement

Overview

Secretary Kerry named Ambassador Nancy Powell to lead the State Department's coordination with other federal agencies and outreach to international partners, including foreign governments. Ambassador Powell's efforts are being supported by an Ebola Coordination Unit (ECU). The Diplomatic Engagement funding in this request supports programmatic efforts across the affected region that largely aligns with "Pillar III, Coherent Leadership and Operations" described previously, and provides funding for Contributions to International Organizations that supports "Pillar I, Control the Outbreak".

Summary Table – Emergency Ebola Request Levels

Accounts ($ in thousands)	FY 2013 Actual	FY 2014 Estimate	FY 2015 Request (As Amended as of 11/5/2014)	FY 2015 Emergency Request	FY 2015 Revised Request
Diplomatic Engagement	**7,845,415**	**7,884,924**	**8,301,159**	**71,420**	**8,372,579**
Diplomatic & Consular Programs	6,467,426	6,617,625	6,782,510	35,420	6,817,930
Contributions to International Organizations	1,376,338	1,265,762	1,517,349	35,000	1,552,349
Repatriation Loans Program Account	1,651	1,537	1,300	1,000	2,300

Diplomatic & Consular Programs (D&CP): $35.4 million

Office of the Medical Director (MED): $32.3 million D&CP
The Office of the Medical Director is requesting $32.3 million in Emergency FY 2015 D&CP funds. The Office of Medical Services is responsible for the overall medical program within the Department of State, serving the entire official U.S. government overseas community operating under Chief of Mission authority.

Air Ambulance medical evacuation of U.S. government Ebola Viral Disease (EVD) patients: $25 million
Unlike prior viral hemorrhagic fever outbreaks that typically occur in sparsely populated villages, this epidemic has spread to major population centers in four countries, dramatically increasing the number of infections and complicating containment of the disease. Several thousand American citizens currently reside in the affected countries, with several hundred involved in battling the outbreak directly. There are currently over 300 U.S. government personnel operating in the region under Chief of Mission authority - as such, the Department's Office of Medical Services is responsible for developing and maintaining mechanisms for medical evacuation should these personnel fall victim to EVD infection. The medical evacuation of patients infected with CDC Category A (Highly Contagious) pathogens requires specifically engineered and approved isolation capabilities. It is imperative that the Department maintain a responsive and rapidly deployable medical evacuation capability to support this crisis.

The Department currently holds the contract with the sole company capable of providing aeromedical biological containment evacuation services, thus, the U.S. government is the only government capable of providing this service. This contract is to transport patients with suspected or confirmed EVD infection, as needed. As the U.S. government and international response expands into West Africa, the Department finds itself in a number of reimbursable agreements for evacuation services with the governments of Canada, Norway, the Netherlands, Switzerland, and Australia, as well as with the World Health Organization and the European Commission's Humanitarian Aid and Civil Protection Department (ECHO) and expects demand to continue with other nations and international organizations entering into similar reimbursable agreements. At the request of the National Security Council and the urging of the inter-agency partners, the Department will expand its capability from one aircraft to two, anticipating up to five Ebola missions per month. Without fully funding this requirement, the Department, the U.S. government, and the international community is at risk of losing the only asset currently capable of long-distance medical evacuation with bio-containment.

Medical evacuation support for non-EVD Infected State Department patients: $6.3 million
The epidemic of EVD in Western Africa has severely impacted MED's use of traditional aero medical evacuation resources. Travel restrictions imposed by vendors have made typical urgent medical evacuations in Liberia, Guinea, Sierra Leone, and Nigeria (because of its proximity to the Ebola-affected countries) impossible. Additionally, airports in cities such as Dakar and Accra, which normally serve North America and Europe, have restricted flights originating from countries currently combatting the EVD. This request will allow for MED to procure other evacuation assets and services so that Department employees in West Africa with non-Ebola Virus Disease medical emergencies can be transported to neighboring countries.

MED is currently in contact with several regional aero evacuation vendors in West Africa who are willing to fly into countries dealing with the EVD to assist with the evacuation on non-EVD patients. These vendors can transport patients into a regional safe haven such as Bamako, Mali to transfer that patient to an awaiting dedicated aero medical evacuation flight to Europe or North America. These air bridges are estimated to cost $2,700,000.

In addition to Temporary Travel Duty (TDY) and other costs of establishing the air bridge, MED is faced with a significantly increased cost in medical evacuation alone. In the past, many patients requiring urgent medical evacuation could be flown aboard scheduled commercial carriers. Due to heightened health security measures at local and regional airports, increased border security, and decreased commercial airline services, the Department's previous lower-cost air evacuation options are no longer available. These posts are now forced to use a dedicated air ambulance for transportation, with many cases being routed to the continental United States because the traditional hubs in London and Pretoria cannot find a hospital willing to accept the patient for fear of EVD. Estimated costs related to these new restrictions are $3.6 million.

Personal Protective Equipment: $350,000
The introduction and unprecedented spread of EVD in West Africa has forced a reevaluation of the PPE posture in high-risk posts. In order to keep pace with evolving CDC and WHO guidance regarding PPE requirements for biological threats, and to build a small capability to care for an official American while awaiting medical evacuation, MED must select, procure, field, and train staff to use new protective equipment. Without these resources, diplomatic posts are left vulnerable to infection and the spread of EVD within the embassy community.

Temporary Duty Travel (TDY): $520,000
As the fight against EVD continues, and MED supports the growing international response to contain the disease, MED must also keep Health Units open with seamless coverage, reinforce the Health Units during surges of international response, and provide frequent and consistent subject matter expertise to interface with the providers on the ground, the post leadership, and the international community. All will require extensive temporary duty travel at significant but unavoidable cost. Without the ability to support the Department's health providers in the field, and provide representation and leadership internationally, the Department's efforts will be significantly diminished.

Contract Nurse: $150,000
MED is seeking to retain a contract nurse to support the Health Unit in Monrovia. Over the coming months, Government employees from various U.S. government agencies such as CDC, DoD, U.S. Public Health Service, etc. will continue to arrive in Monrovia. The Health Unit in Monrovia, which is currently staffed by a While Actually Employed (WAE) Regional Medical Officer and two local nurses, does not have the capacity to care for these new arrivals. In order to provide adequate service to these new arrivals and also care for the existing Embassy staff, MED must increase the staffing level at the health unit. The funding request will allow MED to hire a contract Registered Nurse for one year.

Bureau of African Affairs (AF): $2.2 million D&CP
The Bureau of African Affairs is requesting $1.7 million in emergency FY 2015 D&CP funds to support the Ebola Coordination Unit (ECU) and the AF posts most impacted by the Ebola virus outbreak crisis. The request is composed of the following:

Contractor support of Ebola Coordination Unit and AF Domestic Offices: $950,000
In the past few months, the Bureau of African Affairs has been tasked to staff the Nigeria Policy and Operations Group, the Security Governance Initiative, and the Africa Peacekeeping Rapid Response Partnership. This has strained existing staffing resources, and the Bureau will require additional support in coordinating the Department's outreach and response.

Travel costs for the ECU: $250,000
The ECU staff will be traveling to the affected countries to oversee, coordinate and monitor the Department's response to the Ebola virus outbreak. Team members will also be required to travel to conferences to coordinate the international relief effort.

WAE and TDY travel costs to target countries (Sierra Leone, Liberia, and Guinea, and others as necessary): $500,000
The Department is utilizing in-house as well as WAE resources to provide surge staffing support to the most affected posts. These staff will enhance the management and administrative platforms at these posts as they are tasked to provide support to a large surge in TDYers from USAID, CDC, DoD, and other U.S. government agencies responding to the Ebola virus outbreak crisis. Without this assistance, these embassies' small management platforms will be quickly overwhelmed.

The Bureau of African Affairs is also requesting $500,000 in Emergency FY 2015 Public Diplomacy funds for Ebola virus outreach and programming. The Bureau of African Affairs/Public Diplomacy and Public Affairs anticipates employing a three-pronged strategy to undertake programming, outreach, and education with respect to Ebola. The request is composed of the following (in priority order):

Public Diplomacy programs and engagement: $400,000
Funds would allow posts (currently Sierra Leone, Liberia, and Guinea, and others as necessary) to expand and enhance current engagement and programming on the Ebola virus, enabling post to build on early successes and continue critical efforts to educate affected populations and counter misinformation. Because of high illiteracy rates, programs would include the creation and broadcast of programs, including songs and videos on Ebola virus dangers and prevention. Programs will incorporate the use of art and drama to target youth audiences with the Ebola virus outbreak messaging and personal outreach to traditional leaders to deliver messages on reducing the spread of the disease. These messages will be tailored to reach rural and urban audiences. The Bureau is utilizing in-house as well as WAE resources to provide surge staffing support to the most affected posts (currently Sierra Leone, Liberia, and Guinea, and others as necessary). In addition to supporting Public Affairs Officers (PAOs) in the affected countries (two of the current posts are single-PAO posts), AF plans to deploy communication experts to develop strategic communication, organize crisis communications, work with the media, utilize education and social media, where appropriate, to counter rampant misinformation. The intention is to

control the messaging on the Ebola virus. This is especially important where countries may have serious credibility problems with the general population and cannot communicate an effective message which counters bad information.

<u>Outreach with Broadcasting Board of Governors/Voice of America (VOA): $100,000</u>
This would be a continuation of ongoing VOA efforts supported by the Department. Pursuant to an FY 2014 inter-agency transfer agreement, VOA provided news coverage and reporting of the outbreak and U.S. efforts to help contain it. With these funds, media content generated by VOA would continue to be distributed via television, radio, and digital (social media/web) on VOA language services in the region.

Bureau of International Security and Nonproliferation (ISN): $900,000 D&CP
To support the administration of $5.3 million in NADR-GTR programs in the context of a highly dynamic and unpredictable outbreak, the Department requests $900,000 in Diplomatic and Consular Programs (D&CP) funding to support four additional personnel. These civil service term appointment personnel will ensure the Department is able to effectively execute and oversee these vital activities, and carry out associated diplomatic engagement with partner countries to facilitate the expeditious implementation of this assistance.

Contributions to International Organizations: $35 million

Funding is urgently needed to enable the United Nations to address the Ebola crisis. This request for $35 million would provide for the U.S. share of assessed contributions to the UN regular budget for support to the UN Mission for Emergency Ebola Response (UNMEER). The United States share of these contributions is 22 percent. Other UN member states will be responsible for the remaining 78 percent of the UNMEER's costs, which the Department currently estimates to be approximately $160 million through the end of calendar year 2015.

At the request of the General Assembly, the UN Secretary-General established UNMEER to lead the response at the operational level and provide strategic direction to the United Nations system and other implementing partners on the ground that are addressing the Ebola crisis in western Africa. This request only covers the U.S. share of the estimated amount of UN regular budget funding that will go to support UNMEER. Governmental and non-governmental donors are funding other UN entities through voluntary contributions directly to those entities or to a multi-partner trust fund established for the purpose of distributing funding to entities other than UNMEER.

UNMEER has five broad strategic priorities: stopping the spread of the disease; treating the infected; ensuring essential services; preserving stability; and preventing the spread of the disease to countries currently unaffected. UNMEER is drawing on the technical capabilities and expertise of the existing UN presence in the area. The UN entities participating in the effort include the World Health Organization, the World Food Program, the United Nations Children's Fund, and the UN Office for the Coordination of Humanitarian Affairs.

UNMEER is the first United Nations emergency health mission. In an initial report describing the mission, the Secretary-General proposed that it include 283 short-term contractors. Roughly one third of these positions are at UNMEER's headquarters in Accra. Most of the remainder of the positions are in the three countries currently affected: Guinea, Liberia, and Sierra Leone. While the mission is being staffed immediately with personnel on short-term loan, there will be further scrutiny and decisions of the staffing structure in the UN Advisory Committee on Administrative and Budgetary Questions and the General Assembly's Fifth Committee, which has responsibility for decisions on administrative and budgetary matters.

Funding for UNMEER also helps to provide the necessary infrastructure to enable the mission to perform its tasks. The infrastructure includes facilities, air transportation, ground transportation, information communications technology, and supplies, services, and equipment. UNMEER's infrastructure would complement and leverage infrastructure that already exists in-country because of the presence of other UN entities, notably the World Food Program and the United Nations Children's Fund.

UNMEER officials have indicated that they plan to create approximately ten forward logistical bases to push Ebola relief supplies out closer to ETUs and CCCs in the field. Strategic airlift will be used to bring supplies and equipment directly into the capitals of the three affected countries, from where they will immediately be transported to these logistical bases and onward to the ETUs. UNMEER officials plan to mobilize an international effort that will eventually extend to 369 CCCs and 60 ETUs across the three affected countries.

UNMEER's responsibilities will also extend to non-affected countries. The Secretary-General will provide further specifics on UNMEER's responsibilities and resource needs in a report to the General Assembly in late November. That report will provide the basis for further review and a decision by the General Assembly on resource levels for calendar year 2015. The General Assembly has authorized expenditures of up to $49.9 million for the time frame September through December 2014.

Repatriation Loans Program Account: $1 million
The Department of State requests an additional $1 million for the Repatriation Loan Program Account to finance repatriation loans to U.S. citizens who are exposed to or have contracted the Ebola Virus Disease (EVD). The FY 2015 subsidy rate for the Repatriation Loan Program of 52.65 percent will enable a loan level of $1,899,335.

The current EVD outbreak emergency could significantly impact the Department's existing repatriation funds due to an anticipated increase in the need for repatriation of U.S. citizens from EVD-affected areas. Resources currently available for the repatriation of U.S. citizens with EVD or exposed to EVD are limited. Non-commercial arrangements must be made and there is only one plane equipped to handle patients that already exhibit symptoms of EVD; costs to use this charter carrier are between $180,000 and $250,000 for a single trip. Further, it is quite possible that the Department will be expected to repatriate a private U.S. citizen in need of urgent medical care. Just a few of these cases would significantly deplete the Department's available repatriation funds. Since local resources are already strained, an increasing number of non-EVD patients must also be flown out of West Africa for treatment. In the current environment, even non-EVD repatriations may be problematic, as airlines and air ambulances are not willing to carry the risk of transporting anyone suspected of having EVD.

"No cost" evacuations are exceedingly rare. The Department of State may provide assistance through the repatriation loan account to support individual US citizens. At this time, the vast majority of medical evacuations for private U.S. citizens would require a repatriation loan if the individual lacked sufficient resources for the charter carrier.

Additional administrative expenses are anticipated and those costs would be funded out of the Border Security Program (BSP), as is the case with administrative expenses for other repatriation loans.

Contingency Fund

The Administration is requesting $1.5 billion for a Contingency Fund, with $751 million for HHS and $792 million for USAID and the Department of State. Given the changing nature of the Ebola outbreak, the Contingency Fund is requested to ensure that there are resources available to respond to the evolving situation. If necessary, the Contingency Fund could support increased domestic efforts, such as border screening; an expanded response in Guinea and Sierra Leone; and enhanced global health security efforts. As the rapidly evolving and unpredictable outbreak progresses, it is necessary to have maximum flexibility to respond quickly.

This funding will complement the ongoing efforts to combat the spread of Ebola, including deploying key medical and expert personnel, scaling-up the DoD presence, building a new hospital for infected workers, building Ebola Treatment Units, and reaching out to communities assisting with safe burials. Without these additional resources, agencies will be unable to help control the outbreak, mitigate economic, social and political impacts of the crisis, ensure adequate domestic preparedness, develop safe and effective treatments and vaccines or advance the Global Health Security Agenda. For these reasons, this emergency funding is needed to enhance the Administration's current whole-of-government response to help end the Ebola outbreak in Africa.